THE NATIONAL POETRY SERIES

The National Poetry Series was established in 1978 to ensure the publication of five books annually through participating publishers. Publication is funded by the late James A. Michener, the Copernicus Society of America, Edward J. Piszek, the Lannan Foundation, and the National Endowment for the Arts.

1999 COMPETITION WINNERS

Tenaya Darlington of Wisconsin, *Madame Deluxe*
Eugene Gloria of Massachusetts, *Drivers at the Short-Time Motel*
Corey Marks of Texas, *Renunciation*
Dionisio Martinez of Florida, *Climbing Back*
Standard Schaefer of California, *Nova*

MADAME DELUXE

POEMS

Tenaya Darlington

COFFEE HOUSE PRESS

Minneapolis

COPYRIGHT © 2000 Tenaya Darlington
COVER PHOTOGRAPH © Super Stock
AUTHOR PHOTOGRAPH © André Darlington
COVER + BOOK DESIGN Kelly N. Kofron

COFFEE HOUSE PRESS is an independent nonprofit literary publisher supported in part by a grant provided by the Minnesota State Arts Board, through an appropriation by the Minnesota State Legislature, and in part by a grant from the National Endowment for the Arts. Significant support has also been provided by the Bush Foundation; Elmer L. & Eleanor J. Andersen Foundation; General Mills Foundation; Honeywell Foundation; James R. Thorpe Foundation; Lila Wallace Reader's Digest Fund; Pentair, Inc.; McKnight Foundation; Patrick and Aimee Butler Family Foundation; The St. Paul Companies Foundation, Inc.; the law firm of Schwegman, Lundberg, Woessner & Kluth, P.A.; Star Tribune Foundation; the Target Foundation; West Group ; and many individual donors. To you and our many readers across the country, we send our thanks for your continuing support.

COFFEE HOUSE PRESS books are available to the trade through our primary distributor, Consortium Book Sales & Distribution, 1045 Westgate Drive, Saint Paul, MN 55114. For personal orders, catalogs, or other information, write to: Coffee House Press, 27 North Fourth Street, Suite 400, Minneapolis, MN 55401.

LIBRARY OF CONGRESS CIP INFORMATION
Darlington, Tenaya, 1971–
  Madame Deluxe : poems / by Tenaya Darlington
  p. cm.
  ISBN 1-56689-105-1 (alk. paper)
    I. Title.
    PS3554.A723 M33 2000   2000
    811´.6--DC21   00-043023

                                              CIP

10 9 8 7 6 5 4 3 2

CONTENTS

❧ SEQUINNED, SIZE 16 ❦

❧ PLEATHER MATH ❦

for Snarl

ACKNOWLEDGMENTS

Grateful acknowledgment is made to the editors of the following journals, in which these poems first appeared: *Quarterly West:* "Magnificent Departure" (reprinted as "Velvet Duets"), "He She Van"; *Sonora Review:* "Portrait With No Shortage of History," "On the Catwalks of Desire," "Madame Deluxe's Adult Video and All-Nite Deli"; *The Chronicle of Higher Education:* "Academic Tectonics"; *Southern Poetry Review:* "Madame Deluxe"; *High Beams:* "Aphrodite's Identity Crisis"; *Sun Dog:* "Half-Moons"; *Atlanta Review:* "350-lb. Poem"; *Third Coast:* "Career Cashier," "Not Wanting a Child"; *Wisconsin Academy Review:* "Menona Gives Me Vertigo," "A Student Asks the Poet Basho: What Is Victoria's Secret?"

Vats of thanks to my mentors: Sonja Darlington, Mahlon Darlington, Carl Mumm, Mary Swander, Beth Tornes, Alyce Miller, Clint McCown, John Rosenwald, Kirk Daddow, and Sally Beisser. I'd also like to heap gratitude on the MFA program at Indiana University and on the following individuals for their input, their support, and their glittering cores: Vandanna Khanna, Jen Grotz, David Daniels, Scott Stubbs, Gretchen Knapp, Heather Schroeder, David Ebenbach, Heather Skyler, Dean Bakopoulos, Steve Fay, and Patrick Marley.

Merci to Lawson Inada for selecting this manuscript and to Susan Gubar for uttering "Madame Deluxe."

I drink to drown my sorrows,
but the damn things have learned to swim.

—Frida Kahlo

I've been called Aunt Jemima,
Bitch, Cunt, Dyke,
Exhibitionist,
Fucker, Gook,
Hole,
Idiot, Jezebel,
Kike, Lesbo, Misfit
Nothing,
Oh . . . baby,
Pussy,
Quadroon,
Rudegirl,
Slut, Turboslut,
Urbancowgirl,
Vamp,
Whore,
X-yuppyslut &
Zome other
Yucky, eXistential,
Whacky, Vicious,
Unfounded,
Terribly Sadistic, Rude,
Questionable, Perverted,
Overtly Naziistic,
Misogynistic, Lewd, Kinky, Justplainstupid,
Horrid, Ignorant, Gross, Far-fetched,
Endamaging,
Disgusting,
Closeted,
Bullshit,
And
    so
      I am asking you nicely . . .

CALL ME MADAME DELUXE.

SEQUINNED, SIZE 16

THE BIRTH OF MADAME DELUXE

It didn't start with pains.
No water broke. It started with a pair of glasses,
turtle bone and rhinestones
culled from a heap of old frames:
bent twigs and nose pads
promising a better vision
a way to stand things
in a way I couldn't stand things then,
a sort of trajectory toward the universe.

My purse swung on my arm
like a balance and I knelt down before god's
bifocals on the fecal rug
and drew up this pair: turtle bone, rhinestones.
The prescription was off just enough
to give the world a heavenly haze
and the Sears Tower became covered in glorious shag;
faux fur on everything.

I said *this is it,*
this is it to my beaky friend Terry—
I sez, I am never going out without these.
Crazy how from then on
I saw everything in a two-tone gaze.
Even the hip cats had real tails,
I tell you fuzz is essential. The city is bearable.
A new frame changed the whole Degas
and I saw past every sugary gimmick
into the true glitz bomb.

From that snazz womb
crawled forth Madame Deluxe.
All optometry.
All eyes. Ass first and eager
with rip-roaring hair.

ON THE CATWALKS OF DESIRE

All Karl-Heinz wants is a whippet.
All G. wants is someone who doesn't snore
so she can remove the tampons
from her ears. All the teacher wanted
was to be worshiped like Robert Bly.
All she said was *Robert Bly has a balalaika.*
You just want to be tied up.
M. just wants to move to Chicago with her man
and house-sit for famous writers so she can snoop
through manuscripts and look at their underwear
under the light. All they do is get together and drink
Long Islands on Thursdays
and write a few lines on the back
of a menu. You just wanted me to say yes
to that explicit dream about the ski lodge.
All anybody wants
is to knock off a good poem
by the time they're thirty and maybe appear
in Best American. All P. wants to do is frequent
strip clubs and look for women who remind him
of other women he has known.
All M. ever does is talk
about the great buffets in Reno—mountains of seafood,
racks of cakes, blah, blah, blah.
He just likes to walk around Wal-Mart all day
with his hands in his pockets. She wants cheap flip-flops.
All you ask is that we floss together at night.
All Dave wants is a house
made of straw. All Dennis wants is someone
to share his Camembert. David wants a furniture store
with moon lamps. Secretly, they love to sit
on that god-awful porch drinking American beer

beneath lit fruit. Cath just wants to borrow
a stocking cap to take Lovey for a walk
in the graveyard. You want to do it
without protection. No,
it's not that way. All we want is for someone to get it.
I want someone to have an emotional reaction
to line two, she says. All the poem wants
is for someone to stick their fingers through it
and wear it around town like a mask.
Lovey wants a doughnut.
All anyone really wants is a doughnut.
The doughnut guy wants to buy my earrings
right off my ears to give to his lover;
he'll give me a whole tray of holes.
I just wanted to say hello,
not get backed into the corner by the fridge
for an hour of superficial conversation
about your sister's experience at Bible college.
Alice just wants tenure. Mike just wants
the Vikings to win and maybe a mousy girl to sit
in the beanbag chair by his leg.
All I want to know is where words like *nookie*
and *nougat* come from and if they're derived
from the same root. What root would that be?
All S. ever did was write letter after
letter to a girl he met at science camp, and eventually
they got married. All C. wants to do is hold me
like a baby. We want some chickens and a goat named
Malloy. His dad wants
him to be a dentist, not an academic,
least of all a poet. All they want to do
is write this sort of thing.

350-LB. POEM

My sisters appear in monosyllabic bikinis
nibbling haiku on beds of lettuce,
bulimic blank verse girls
and centerfolds of prose
wearing short words and skimpy devices.
You run your fingers down their soft vowels,
across their slender stanza bones,
watching the line breaks break-dance
across the page on Dexatrim.
Remember,
they are only figures of speech,
lying out on the page, slathered in sunscreen,
wearing punctuation marks that barely cover
their assonance.
They part their titles
and kiss your villanelle.
I, on the other hand, with my appetite
for date-filled description,
bite rotund adjectives
and bloat paragraphly.
I down the lexicon whole,
snarf a raw thesaurus,
lick the spell-checker,
binge between dark pages,
and break out in boils and ballads.
I put on bulky clothing
to cover up my large vocabulary
and try to appear
in small print.

MADAME DELUXE'S
ADULT VIDEO & ALL-NITE DELI

Here's a preview:
the universe seems tender.
Love has reached epidemic proportions,
beyond jean brand or bra size,
but at its epicenter, there is only
shelf life and viewing time to consider.

This is a comedy: many modern films
end on "light" because
its letters are tall and bosomy.

This is family / revenge:
the laws of gravity turn
a couple of teenage girls
into a bunch of vampire blood-slaves
who retain moral integrity.

This is a tragedy:
you strip away the leather,
and the dominatrix
is covered in shoulder pads.

This is a romance:
    You love you.
This is a heartwarming coming-of-orgy:
    You love you.
    The critics love you.

Here's a scene from tonight's pick:
Garçon,
even this glass of H_2O can be life-
threatening.

Ebert says: once a sex fiend, always a sex fiend.
Two thumbs up. The moral hierarchy turns
the laws of gravity
into the laws of detachment.
Guffaw, guffaw.

Gene remains grave,
shrink-wrapped in the cooler
of tongues.

APHRODITE'S IDENTITY CRISIS

Love is Greek to me now.
On earth there are only personals,
couples banking on the internet
sans pheromones or fishnets.
High heels click a mouse-click away.
The fastest zip drive beats
fine lingerie. Control, Alt, Delete,
and you Escape without apology.
Dot Com is the girl du jour
just a button away.
Would that I understood how the hard
drive crashed.

Call me old-fashioned.
I was born from foam.
Can't comprehend this system
of starless dating,
a crowded earth of carping hearts
encased in complex housing—
What font is this?
What shortcut but to oneness?
Fingers tapping ether.
The body mooned
to a moistureless keyboard,
passwords long forgotten.

From Olympus, Eros and I
watch every season on our loveseat.
As the world turns,
yearning forms a great gas cloud.
The young and the restless suffer
from sorrows deeper than the Styx.
Desire is but an ember

the lucky remember prior
to the digital fix, when hearts hung
in great bunches
commanded by Morpheus.
Then there was dancing,
aphrodisia, and real arrows
opened the soft, micro-
fibers of each beast's breast.

DOS, Basic, Java,
what languages are these? What romance
breeds between usernames
but bitter wanderlust?
What fax machine
delivers an inkless kiss?
What disk knows the drive?
Hackers fumbling through infinity,
pirating libidos,
to download virginity.
Has paradise come to this:
Two screens on a secluded beach
sending static each to each?

VENUS, I DON'T NEED YOU

Sex life in the Paleolithic must have been quite unerotic,
for this Venus was no more than a lump of fat.
—from *Sex in History.*

Let's face it, Venus,
you're kinda chunky. You may very
well be Botticelli's idea of a good time, but venerate
you I will not. I know
every poet from Virgil to Vaughan has versified
your beauty. But besides being a veritable
floozy and a heavyweight vixen
you're hardly a viable centerfold. Not that you aren't virtuous
(though you were the patron saint of harlots—a vocation
I wouldn't vaunt) but those Paleolithic figurines, from my vantage
point, verge on vulgar.
I would venture
to say perhaps the artist exaggerated your "vestigial"
features (either viciously or with vim),
but your ever-blooming volume
is not going to cut the Viennese Torte (which, by the way, is verboten
if you want to fit into this year's Calvins).
Venus, the stringy hair must go. Your thighs give me vertigo.
Your breasts look too volatile, your rear too viscous.
A nose job is inevitable, liposuction investigable.
Eventually, with enough vigorous exercise, maybe Versace
could veer you toward something voguish in black velvet.
Then you could sit vis á vis Kate Moss and sip vintage
wine, reminiscing vaguely about virginity
to the backdrop of Vivaldi and handfuls of Valium.
Oh Venus, evolve or dissolve. Beauty has gone virtual
and virtually no one is interested in *your* notion of voluptuous.

MADAME DELUXE'S
MAIL-ORDER BRIDES

i. Ordering Your Bride

To order, simply send check or credit card information
along with your saliva sample and a clean dress to the address
listed below. Our brides are among the most widely circulated
brides in the world. No more matchmaking
or back-alley deals. Your soul mate will be hand-selected
from a variety of flawless family trees,
plucked from deep sleep, wrapped in burlap, then RUSHED
to you in a hermetically sealed box to prevent aging or tampering.
If you are not completely satisfied, simply remove dress
and return your bride for a full refund.

No more waiting.
And best of all, no more cold shoulders.

ii. Receiving Your Bride

Open box carefully. Do not use letter opener or knife to cut tape,
as packing peanuts may have settled during shipping and contents
may have shifted. Unwrap your bride carefully, removing gauze
from ears and eyelids. To revive your bride, simply run hands and feet
under warm water. If your bride is slow to revive or feels dry to the touch,
spritz gently with one part rosewater, two parts goat's milk.
If your bride stutters at first, place a cricket under her tongue.
Depending on the flexibility of your bride, it may take one to two weeks
for her to completely unfurl and walk without the assistance of a staff.

iii. Asking For Her Hand

Once you have developed a rapport with your new Deluxe Bride,
you may ask for her hand. If she says no, you must accept
another appendage. Under no condition should you sever
the hand of your bride or otherwise desecrate her publicly.
Brides are bribe-resistant and not susceptible to reprimands.

iv. How To Endear Your Bride To You Forever

Tell her she looks lean as a sparerib.
Layer her bath with the skin of kiwis.
Do not ask about her ancestors or make her the subject of your alchemy.
Do not castrate bulls in front of her.
Do not put hot fish in her navel.
Buy her exotic spices and reddish-yellow lotions for her skin.
Moisten her lips with royal jelly.
Clean her parts with a soft-bristled scouring brush.
Use ribbed condoms for her pleasure.

v. How To Tell If Your Bride Is Fertile

It is recommended that the husband fill one cloth purse with barley seeds
and the other with salt. Pass her water on them every day.
If, after a week, they neither melt nor sprout,
she will not give birth at all.
Or serve her warm watermelon
pounded and bottled with the milk of a woman
who has borne a son. If your bride vomits,
she will bear. If she belches, she will never bear.

vi. What To Do If Your Bride Is Oversexed

If your bride expects intercourse more than three times a week
or seems preoccupied with quantity, dress her in a white tunic
and force her to feed on custard pie
till there is a contemptuous look in her eye.

vii. What To Do If You Suspect Your Bride Is Unhappy

When your bride is asleep, remove her Deluxe tongue.
Turn it over in your hand. Count the bumps.
Even means happy.
Odd means you have miscounted. Check again.

viii. What To Do If You Suspect Your Bride Is Lying

If you suspect your bride is lying or cheating,
hold her tongue over a blue flame.
If the tongue says it loves you and you feel it's genuine,
put it back in her mouth.
Otherwise, discard immediately.
Will stain hands and feet.

ix. What Other Husbands Have Said

"Even though Nefertiti continually burns the TV dinners, she's
a real ham."

"Jezebel has a short fuse, but the help just love her. She's been
a great addition to the farm."

"Last year Sappho came in a brown box with no identity. Just
like Barbie. This year she shaved her head and started wearing
suit jackets. Just like Ken."

x. The Marriage

Simply peel silver backing off Heavenly Veil (see enclosed) and
apply to bride's forehead. Garters and rings sold separately.

ACADEMIC TECTONICS

I used to live on the other side,
in the front row of the universe.
I took notes like most people write love letters
and believed that the man with the dry erase marker
had an even more dry erase head
which wrote even in its sleep and drew information
like moths to a light. And I believed the other professors
took out their brains at night
and set them in jars to soak up the readings.
Information was a powder like Crystal Light,
made of mysterious ions.
Add two heaping spoonfuls to water and stir
till all of European history dissolves.
How else could they remember so much?
How else could their heads hold
so many allusions and equations?
The brain on the nightstand absorbing Chaucer like a sponge,
the whole lexicon fizzing like two tablets in the bottom of the glass.
By morning, each pink brain rich
as angel food cake doused in a familiar liqueur.

On the other side,
on the other side, I roamed among classrooms at night,
snagging on shadows. A few offices still lit
as if sheer brilliance ignited the desks. File cabinets on fire.
With my backpack, I was carrying my house around
the way a snail does, or a turtle, each book a small trailer.
Occasionally I found a door unlocked,
slipped inside, stood at the front of the dark auditorium
before an audience of chairs. The moon—
the only light shining through the window,
just as mysterious as the night before,
and casting a pall across the carpeted floor
like a faint spotlight, not quite a spotlight,
but the dream of one to come.

Now I swivel in my swivel chair,
officially my throne through office hours,
slip through the numbers of *my* syllabi,
and equate hours with pages
and evenings with readings.
My desk sags under paper's weight
and time both well and ill spent.
The mystery of knowledge is the mystery
of keeping it fresh, ziplocked
and totable. I dream of my own brain
drying out like a loofah
in an empty shower. There is no such
powder with all of history
in each grain, and the only way to remember
the greatest poems is to say them
day after day, year after year
to a classroom of students,
as if they came off the top of my head.

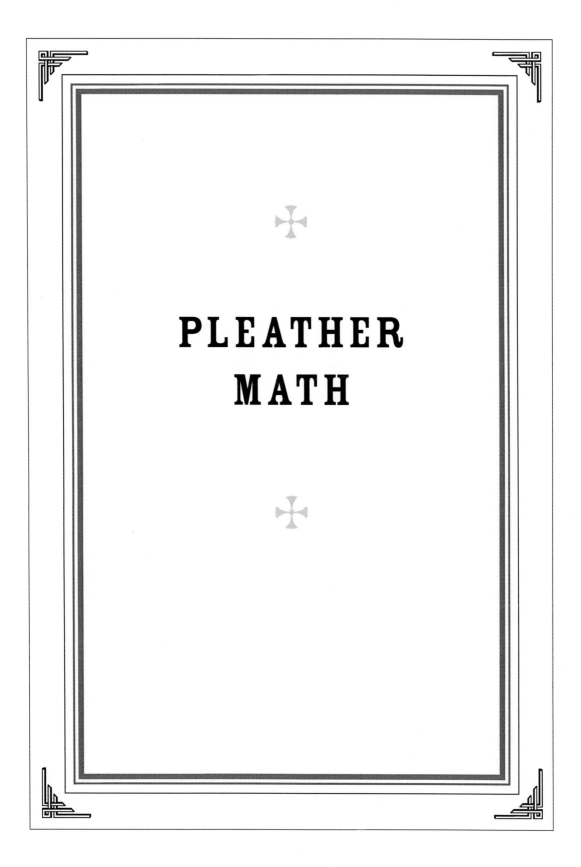

PLEATHER
MATH

FROM OOLONG TO OOMPAH

A thin, lightweight, translucent
person opens
continuously, issuing an immature
egg through a doorway
paid for by the host
regardless of metaphysics (loosely:
the assertion that God was conceived of
in a brown amber tea,
an open and shut case
free of navigational hazards
not stopped by a finger. The final
syllable was surgically removed
from a dome-like roof).
Now, a one-woman show opens
its door to the public
to uncover, to lay bare,
to render a causeway
between romance
languages: the jet-black gem resembling music, opera
set in a deep-bodied bog.
A bulb,
a large, pungent onion
comes into view
and turns the pages of a book.
Amateurs and professionals
may compete
but there has long been a tendency
to place ONLY before each verb.
Somewhere in space,
in a city that is officially declared "accessible,"
        a box ending in a vowel
                moves toward shore
where an only child,
of an iridescent variety,
utters or exclaims *ooooh*
aware of true nature.

MADAME DELUXE'S GUIDE
TO THE PLEASURES OF LEATHER

On a first date, wear oiled nubuck ankle boots.

On a blind date, a low-heeled mule.

If he is late, switch to saw-toothed soles with aggressive rubber bottoms.

If you feel jumpy, a monk-strap buckle loafer.

When you feel trapped, oyster-textured crocodile.

To insulate the heart, gum-rubber.

To rebuff the claws of Cancer, unassuming flats.

To rouse the head of Leo, anything with zippers.

Pick a lug sole, a square toe. When you can't say no.

To say yes: stilettos.

Suede, if the answer is maybe.

If he seems duplicitous, have your moccasins handy.

If he wants to fly you in his Leer jet to Vegas,
Put your slip-off scuffs on stand-by.

If he says *I truly love you,*
I want you to be mine forever,
I throw myself at your feet:

Kick off your shoes and walk all over him.

MENONA GIVES ME VERTIGO

Boulders along the canal form a bucktooth shore.
A man carrying his leather jacket

is a man whose hand has become a crow.
Along the opposite shore, a sailboat is anchored

at an empty table—
one plate with an expertly-folded napkin.

Women in bikinis, like old hors d'oevres
garnished with slivers of radish, look up

as a distant motorboat approaches: an otter
drags a lost veil, the light toppling.

So the nest above me is a brain craving a body.
The trees and their shadows reminisce about dark

tangled bedding, but the waves—
they bring the undergarments back:

scarves, slips, all that we have lost
wading. At this hour,

the columbines have not been lit;
reeds along the shore stir

like hats of submerged women
drinking port below the surface.

Even the fishermen along the banks at dusk
reel in one long clear hair after another

but rarely win love back.

TREND-CASTER

You comb every groove for a boom,
predict the next hot dish, fax it ASAP
to the corporate reps.

I imagine you with a gizmo like a metal detector—
one of those old people beneath bleachers
combing their hunch for booty.
You would stop on a word like that,
the apparatus buzzing around a lingual fad.
Boom: it's tube tops
and skirts cut like sacks.
Next year's colors will be gravy and snow.

Boom: martinis are the wet dreams
of jet-setting DINKS (Double Income No Kids—
everybody knows that, as I was told by some poet sans decorum
at a party last week.)
I thought about predictability
as I ate goat cheese, ahem, *chévre.*

What if poets relied on predictions—whole collections
anticipated by designers:
next year's poems will see shorter lines,
with less anaphora.
As you can see, the high-slit stanza
complements the title
with a beautiful double entendre.
Maybe it's happening already
which is why so many poems
are written about blackberries and end on "absence"
after repeating a woman's name
twice in the third-to-last line.

Fashion being an equation, poetry
is geekier math. All the Whitmans
and Frosts are down at the docks,
trolling the beaches,
pawing at the dreck in their dungarees
for a single washed-up buck
or a word—one word
that is still sacred and bright.

TO TASTE

It should really have its own set of legs.
If not legs, then cilia.
There should be some sort of sheath or a thin piece of paper
To keep it from touching the roof of the mouth.
It should sit like a leaf on its bed of teeth or be a decorative
    beetle pinned to bluish tissue.
It should not look like the inner tube of a plum.
When it turns blue, it should be removed like a petal.
In the mirror, it should not try to touch the nose, or pose as
    an unborn thumb.
It should not have the caption, "pluck me, pluck me."
When it licks a stamp, it should not move like a slug pining
    for dew.
When used as an implement for licking the lip, it should not
    repeat itself.
Delis should not serve them.
Vegetarians should be exempt from having them at all.
It should fold up like a bath mat stored in the corner.
It should come in other colors and thinner thicknesses.
It should keep to the cheek during literary references,
And only come out at night.

MADAME DELUXE'S INSTRUCTIONAL MANUAL AND MARRIAGE GUIDE

for the Year 2000

Q. Why does my husband overheat?

A. When your husband is plugged into a wall outlet for his first time or when you resume power after a power interruption, his head may become temporarily scrambled and fail to function as programmed. Unplug him from the wall socket and then plug him back in. He will be resexed for functioning.

Q. Why do I see a reflection around my wife's outer case?

A. The light is from the bulb located inside her birth cavity. Do not use this cavity for storage purposes. Do not store combustible items such as bread, cookies, or paper products inside her. If lightning strikes the power line, she may turn on by herself.

Q. Why does my husband burst?

A. Your husband may be slightly heavier than others, or he may burst due to steam buildup inside his adam's apple, causing his head to swell and expand during the thought process. Steam is naturally produced during talking. If you're concerned, simply pierce his tongue with a toothpick while he is sleeping.

Q. Why does my wife pop?

A. This is caused by her temper. As she becomes angry, she conducts heat and her insides continue cooking during standing time. Use a larger utensil than usual and wear oven mitts to remove her.

Q. How do I know if I'm using my husband properly?

A. This type of husband is specifically designed to heat, cook, and collect food. He is not designed for industrial purposes or laboratory use.

Q. How do I know if I am using my wife correctly?

A. As with most appliances, close supervision is necessary to reduce the risk of a fire in her internal cavity. Do not store her outdoors. Do not use your wife near water, near a kitchen sink, in a wet basement, and the like. Do not let her cord hang over the edge of the table.

Q. What is wrong when our marriage has no spark?

A. There may be several reasons why your marriage has lost its glow:

    1. The light bulb has burned out.

    2. START has not been touched.

ANATOMY OF MELANCHOLY

Celestial influences affect the earth, define the surface,
the death and resurrection of temperament:
a kind of wind that either wails or wheezes dormant.

The everyday is a kind of sickness
borne on winged germs
that wax fanatic and wane supine, leaving the heart

detached from its grotto or hanging
like meat for dogs
from an anachronistic rib.

The first real horoscope was invented by poets,
then mathematicians took over
to name the humors of the human condition,

the rise and fall of opposition.
Tensions measured in terms of curves
named after luxuriant gods.

The horizon's height was considered and plotted
to learn the ways of the heart.
When Scorpio haunts the northern helm

earth dramatizes his rot.
Seeds in their pods are cross-eyed lovers
who can't make their way through the soil.

The child whose breath gets drawn from this sky
will have a sex drive obsessed with death.
Interlocking sub-schemes rule the body,

the heavenly chemistry bubbles over
in the bedrooms of the sky's twelve houses.
Faith is not enough. Prayer is just a suckling dream.

When your neck hurts, if you're glib,
Taurus is restless in the cosmos; bones ache because
Capricorn is ascending; you can't breathe

because Gemini is in transit; your kidney fails
because Libra is screwing an angel.
Illness is hatred spoken through bone.

The body's luminosity is measured in phlegm.
All planetary substances are drawn in carnal vehicles
with the sun as the spirit's chauffeur.

What does all this mean?
Plants that bear fruit should be harvested on a full moon
and tubers sown when the sun is low?

Bad thoughts should be mown
when Mercury is rising and desire unleashed
under Scorpio? Galileo would have said

depression was too much moon in one's map.
Copernicus would have said that yearning
was a matter of orbit. So be it.

One may regard the cell as a prison,
but are not the planets the inmates
of our psyche's prognosis?

Nebulous testimonies based on a chart,
a calendar of deities swooping into hearts
like tsetse flies in divine disguise—wings nothing more than math.

Now Dionne Warwick can channel the devil;
has not the human body won
over the celestial one?

The food chain, a kind of bracelet now.
Astrology a lurid sitcom. The heavens
a sort of campground.

The body in the mirror does not need Venus and Mars
as long as there are uppers in the cupboard:
not 9 but 36 heavenly orbs

resting on a firm cloud of cotton.

DELUXE CREATIONS

I am interested in superstitions,
the structure of the universe, not as atoms
but as four classes of shadowy worlds
where human souls are controlled by deities
not unlike *Star Trek*. You may say
Spock does not belong in a poem
but I am making a case for the supernatural—
not whether it really exists
but how we, like the Eskimo,
can derive a moral order from a legendary past
by imagining afterworlds and otherworlds,
where the ghosts of caribou roam in herds.
Clearly there is a striking connection
between the quality of personal behavior on earth
and individual destiny in the afterlife.
The Eskimo believed in a moon spirit;
and if you were a man who was clever and fast
or a woman with beautiful tattoos,
you could enter the highest chamber,
dine on endless seal meat in a world-class condo.
There was a second world for less skilled hunters
and women with fewer designs. Under the tundra,
there was great fishing but no view.
And in the third world, at the core of the earth,
idle hunters hung their heads,
huddled beside women afraid of needles.
The moon let them starve and go blind.
When she felt generous, she sent down a butterfly.
I am not making a joke out of Darwin or promoting hunting
or tattoos. I am saying that now we can grow two acres
of human skin in a lab. We grow whole hands, even hearts.
Each scientific discovery, crazy enough to be legend,
destroys the myths a little more.
The unicorn can be engineered, the zephyr cloned.
Listen,

at first there was darkness
or a kind of twilight all around.
Some believed people and animals
shared one tongue. Words had great power.
The fox said darkness, darkness.
The hare said day, day.
Because the voice of the hare was stronger,
light was created.

PORTRAIT WITH NO SHORTAGE OF HISTORY

For a while, it seemed like you could pull the birds back to your arms, the needle marks from their sharp beaks were at least a modicum of red dwarf stars.

You took your ecstasies literally, never clitorally, and I watched you buy thinner and thinner dresses, each of them hungrier than the one before.

I was raised on your lovers. They came and went from your veins. The Venus flytrap in the window contracted out your mouth and the hairs around your mouth.

This is the day you turn yourself loose and I catch you again.

In the bathroom, palms like water lilies, uppers like alms in the soap dish and downers drowning the dark heart on purpose.

Why you left the window open . . .

The birds have come in. The grosbeaks have slit the sleeves of all your dresses and taken threads back to the trees: every nest a pale pink cap.

Inverse Cinderella: the hearse driven by a dwarf. Your heart was given to a hunter. There are a variety of themes.

I still dream your body in every bathtub, still clean it from my mind with Q-tips. Every flytrap is a mother's mouth burning for something winged

to take her there and bring her back, never having fled. What do angels and minnows have in common? Speed.

I am the road block that makes wounds open. Not a daughter at all, just a voice, a drug, the breath you heard coming.

THE STUDENT ASKS THE POET BASHO: WHAT IS VICTORIA'S SECRET?

1   Eight pairs of sexy panties
so many pathways
to the cherry tree.

2   The bamboo
has two new shoots:
my lover's spaghetti straps.

3   Tonight to drown my longing
I drink sake
from her seamless cups.

4   White birches
along the water.
Women in matching coordinates.

5   In this world
there are straw sandals.
Then there are bedroom slippers.

6   Our time on earth
high-cut brief.

7   From this planet,
the stars only come
in small and extra small.

8   The crows lift from the limbs.
Take off
your black thong.

9   Out of loneliness,
I try on
your blackberry brassiere.

TAR & FEATHER

Let me say this outright:
this poem does not have any birds in it.
It does not have any geese, but it does
have vaginas flying in formation.
In winter, I take all our old bread down to the Yahara River,
feed the fallen women who swim there.
Their names are almost always left out of poems
but you can tell they are hungry—
they come right to shore,
blue dresses hardening in the air,
hair crisp with frost, feet
red and frozen. Overhead, books flap past,
dust jackets puffed with blurbs,
like lightweight down,
and those women look up to see their blouses there.
Shadows of pillows, pillars
of shadow—lipstick staining wings,
beaks pressed into the sleet of an afternoon nap,
postfrolic, postpartum and mortem. Um,
if our dark pasts must have fowl,
let's agree they will not be fragile. Sparrows,
Wrens. Make them screech
owls. Again
and again, I buy the same book,
each page an aviary of exes, lost glances
chalked against some February sky.
Over and under bows, the Self in flight calls
why
      why
            why

THE DRACULA ORCHID

Only a woman with black toenails.
Only a woman with black toenails could wear this slipper,
this dark, strapless trap.

Like a tongueless mouth it gasps down wasps,
then sips—through its stem—the pseudobulb.
Fussiness fused to a single spike,
imagine how it might bite your hand
if you mist its thirsty throat,
how it might slit yours in the shower,
petals found cast across your neck
when the meter man rings the buzzer.

Headlines: *Horror Flower, Girl Slain.*

Stain: there is a blood-soaked bedspread at its center,
the scent of a killer's cologne lingering.
The Mafia fiddle drones. What florist
would FTP this death fugue to my door?

My hands tremble to draw the shades—
to be alone in a room with this dark black bloom
is my tomb, is my tomb.

Sister, sister, is that you?
Is that your shoe in the hall I hear,
your ragged breath I smell,
your lip on my wrist,
your buried head rising on a stalk
before me on the sill? Is this dew?
Is this sad and beautiful dew, these dark pearls
around your neck, the waxy tracks on your arms,
the jet-black jewel of unconsciousness?

Or is this the flora of my lung,
the dark vestigial tongue
lashing for air through a gray vent? Is this the glove
of the last gorgeous blonde
dumped from a Cadillac's trunk
into a bank of February snow?

Is this forgetting?

Is this how the forgotten heart grows,
up through the loam into a green bloom
that flowers a black kiss?

Until the hearse hauls it away,
stay back, children, you will be bitten.
Some new pain opens.

DISCOUNT
SONNETS

VELVET DUETS

$\mathcal{A}$ couple seeks a corner table in a restaurant where they may dine unobserved. Nerice, the wife, is dressed in a green cloak that looks like a large elm leaf. Against the green curtains, she is able to disguise herself. Her husband, whose very skin looks like old clothes, is wearing a shiny jacket—iridescent blue—like a set of rudimentary wings. After the first course, the waiter notices that their reproductive appendages have appeared. By the time the second course arrives, the husband has discarded his old skin and is beginning to form a new one from liquid secreted by certain glands. By the main course, the wife has a very large abdomen and her cloak is more or less crumpled up. The husband's skin turns a beautiful green color with a number of golden spots. Around the room, other diners have begun to take notice. The husband is on all fours, his nails digging into the taupe carpet while his wife, sitting atop him like a float-parade queen, is steadily laying eggs on his back. This is unpalatable and distasteful to the other diners who are not used to open relationships or home births. All around the restaurant, the women change color; the men bristle and emit an unpleasant odor. They do not know what causes this sort of gall, but just the same, they continue to watch, craning to see past the bouquets on tables. By the time the dessert arrives, the whole place is rubbing cloacae. Intermittent gasps drown the violins. Across tables and under tables, mandibles are pressed together. From behind the swinging doors, the cook watches in amazement, admittedly elated. The room finally stills. The stars come out. The diners leave, grabbing jackets off chairs, faces aglow as they enter the night air from the sill.

CAREER CASHIER

I used to live next to this run-down grocery where the motto was: "Cleaner, Friendlier, Better." Run-down women worked there and even more run-down women shopped there. At any given time, most of the cars in the lot were popping with kids. You could get an orange pop for a quarter from the machine and watch drug dealers smoke on hoods, waiting for the pay phone to ring. If this were a song, the refrain would mention beer nuts, tobacco. Picture produce sparkling with flies, cashiers in red housecoats with their names sewn on the pockets. They were veterans, had rung numbers all their lives. Every day, the same cavalry of bottle blondes. So it came as a shock to all when "Linda B." in blue cursive letters was stabbed. All the petty thievery that must have gone on came down to a knife pulled over some Little Debbie's. The place stayed open, but not without due respect. Those women hung black crepe paper through all six aisles. They taped black balloons to the doors. In front of register #1, most shocking of all, they hung her empty red housecoat from two wires. In the Indiana heat, the crepe paper sagged, brushing the tops of dog food bags and cereal. It weaved a saggy path like six slow snakes to the back of the deli. And the ceiling fan near register #1 made the housecoat dance. Filled with air, its empty lungs breathed. Its red arms motioned for no one to come. The register drawer was open, filled with mums.

RANSOM NOTE TO THE OWNER
OF A LOST COCKATIEL

*L*ast night, my neighbor L. came over with your cockatiel on her shoulder. It had a yellow face, strong claws, wing feathers like green bananas. Earlier, I had heard the crows in an uproar. Maybe you raised the window for some air. Maybe you thought you could trust your cockatiel. We stuck it in a lunch box. L.'s son carried it on his knees in the minivan. We drove all over until we came to what we thought was your house—I'd seen a MISSING BIRD sign there Saturday.

Inside the house, there were two middle-aged women, eating what looked to be some sort of game. Cornish Hens perhaps, Love Birds. They led us through a dark hallway to the back porch which looked over a tremendous aviary. Chicken wire was wrapped around a circle of birches. In the center, a pink marble hot tub was filled with debris.

By the time you read this, you will probably have bought another eighty-dollar bird. I just wanted to let you know that I have been visiting your baby. Some evenings, I go in secret to spread the cosmos, peer over the back fence through the trees. I have seen a strange thing: those two women sitting in their hot tub full of leaves, feather masks strapped to their heads. For hours, they chirp back and forth, and your cockatiel looks on, proudly, not the least bit suspicious.

DOMICILES

At the 310 Bistro, we order snails and chew them slow. My father and I with our backs to the lamps, my mother sallow in the corner in her too-bright scarf with the Chinese signature. It's the day after Christmas, the first time we've been together like this in some time, and I think I can distinctly taste the riverbed, the reddish mud where the snails lived happily before becoming elegant hors d'oeuvres. They are served on a bed of rock salt, camouflaged with parsley, yet still perishable-looking and moody.

My mother is too blue to eat them, and I plan on at least two martinis and how I will shove my tongue through the hole in the olive, a compartment like a tongue garage. But the first one never comes—caught between waitresses—that shift between shifts, like the comma between marriages.

So we drink our waters and gorge on slugs, holding their homes with tongs and digging at them with a flared fork. It takes skill and ardor; they are hard to cajole and at some point it seems unethical. *This is like eating an agoraphobic!* My father loves his own joke. My mother looks diminished, opposite us. She studies the wine list, looking for color, pronouncing the names in a whisper. My father, his lips shamelessly buttery, watches a blonde at the next table wiggle out of her coat.

SPREAD

This blood is the same color as the jam I used to eat every morning made of plums. You can see the skins on the bread and later on the napkin. At first, I thought the sweetness was what a girl could die from. My father had to leave the house during a tornado to buy me some pads. We were out and all of us were crouched under the basement stairs with the gray radio. Then I said to my friend Debbie, *walk behind my pants.* In the nurse's office, the diagrams made a uterus look like a tree with eggs that could fall if the wind blew just right, fall right into your hand. Round and ripe, the darkest black. Purple is the color I know best, and sweetness is the taste I recognize when there is something bitter on my tongue. I can smell it later near the toilet, my smell, and the smell of my mother's—her jam, that exact brown with red skins smeared across the blue backseat of the car. In the hospital waiting room, a woman I don't even know lets me put my head in her lap. She calms me down and gives me a sucker with a handle that's a string you pull right down out of yourself.

HE SHE VAN

*Y*our license plate in the parking lot of Aldi: *He she.* Now there, I thought, is a person with real balls. I had only that day been thinking about hermaphrodites— the relatively high percentage born and how the parents must choose. No one ever talks about this, but some of us must be walking around with a secret link to the opposite sex. Like my friend's sister, who developed testicles in her teens and had to have them removed. And to me, the public aside, that seems like a dream, to walk down both sides of the aisle. My body feels, at times, like the wrong garment. Inside me there is this secret compartment, an isle of man. On gray days, I think about dressing up like Vicki C. whose picture is pasted above my stove, crowned and spangled. *Hair and makeup by Jeni-Lyn.* If I were a man, I could dress like a woman and enjoy it. The faux breasts, the false eyelashes, the hips made from foam. How nice to tuck them away at the end of the night, like dark groceries in the door of a dark fridge.

ROSE HILL CEMETERY

——for you, David

This happened in a town almost entirely without doughnuts. One of the first things I noticed: no one ever wants a long john? I moved in with a man I couldn't love and this was a recurring motif. Two years it took us to discover: if you walked down the street of dilapidated bungalows, past the duck dressed like a cop, and through the cemetery—and then, if right by the stone of "Baby Clyde" you scaled the wall—you came to a doughnut shop with a dimly lit vibe.

It went deeper than that. This was the winter neither of us had lovers. We wrote sonnet sequences and played Scrabble to the pastel laughs of "Golden Girls." At night, we fell for anything easy. The first shift of crullers from the 3 A.M. vat. They got to know us down there—Michelle (MEE-shell) and her grubby bodyguard. Bodyguard? Upstairs, you could hear children running, running at that hour.

Cemeteries vary; this one kept a pulse. One night, we walked across a hollow sound and, smoothing away snow, found a plywood board over an empty hole. I wish this hadn't happened: you lowering yourself down, lying in that dark gap. The trees were soft brush marks against the mist. One week earlier, you'd found out you were alive according to some tests. I guess I hadn't realized what that meant.

When you rose from the dead, you replaced the board, brushed off your back, and it hit you then. We walked wordlessly toward desire—the kind of desire that is never in the right form but stands like ice where water should have been. There was a new countergirl, and she led us into the back room where there was a dark man standing before the vat, his forearms floured like casts, a chaw in his cheek like a tumor. Red Man. He jerked on a machine to inflate a bismark with jelly, then let us try, as if we were tourists.

But it was too late. We knew the taste before we licked the hole we were about to fill.

THE DISHES

*O*n the street where I grew up, there was a man whose mother went mad from the rattling of dishes. She was on a train loaded with plates, thousands of plates in stacks. For three solid days, clink clink clink. The train was headed for Auschwitz.

The son, our neighbor, escaped to the u.s. where he studied to be a potter. He built a studio off the back of his house. As a child, I liked to watch him throw, transfixed by the way gray lumps became saucers, bowls, demitasses. Before each firing, he spent the night in his kiln, seated, burning a kind of incense I could smell through the window.

The man was also a marvelous chef, and one night he had my family to dinner. I remember the food was simple: borscht, dark bread, and for dessert: cheese. The discussion was lively; the man was a great teller of jokes, but in his long beard there were hunks of clay. Sitting next to him, I noticed a fine layer of gray dust covered his skin, as if he had just come from the ground. Afterward, he insisted on doing all the dishes. In the cupboard, between each plate, there was a layer of purple velvet.

Years have passed. I'd almost forgotten about the man until a few nights ago when I was awakened by rattling dishes. In the cupboards, mugs clanked against the lips of others, plates quaked despite their shape, bowls shook their roundness loose. In the apartment above ours, new neighbors have moved in—newlyweds. Their bed is right above our kitchen.

My husband sleeps right through, but I get up. In the dark, I lay down on the counter, my head near the bread boards, my feet touching the fridge. I close my eyes and feel the counter enter the switchyards. A distant whistle blows. The plates rattle on, and I peer through a slit to gaze at the obscene shape of the moon.

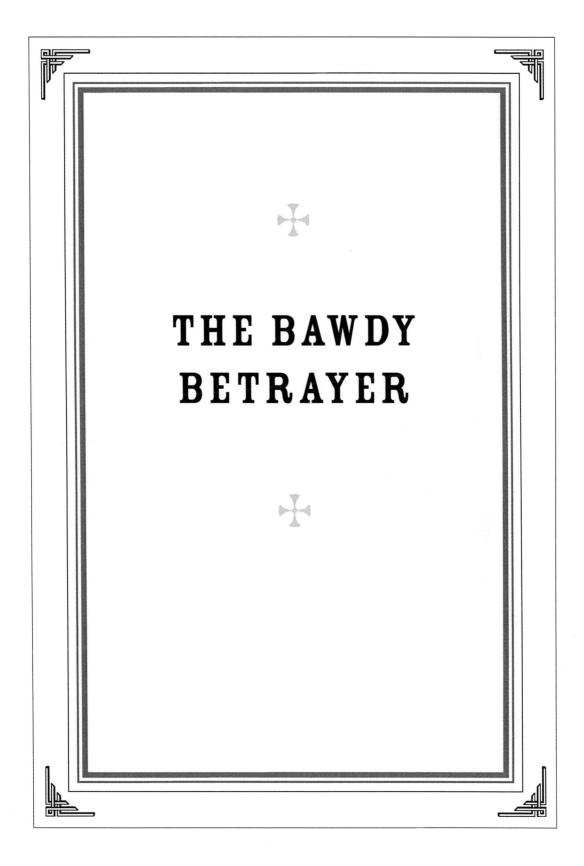

THE BAWDY
BETRAYER

HALF-MOONS

Once I had a clean mouth
and a pink tongue propped in it
like a good liver.

I used a lot of words
like: sentinel, memorabilia,
and pleasantry. Once I was an infant

and perfect teeth
came up out of the gums
like smiling heads—

without caps, without crowns.
People used the word *nice*
and hung it over me

like a couch cover.
And to my mother
they said, *so so sweet.*

All I had to do was eat corn
on the cob in straight lines
'til the summer was over.

I had read all the Bible
stories my mother assigned
and drawn pictures of Delilah

and Samson. My parents
were proud of my portraits,
my tough enamel—the spectacular,

gleaming jaws of their girl.
Virgins are good things,
and I know hundreds

of aspiring actresses. Once I lay
awake at night
just touching my teeth.

I bit my arms until the sun came
through the sheers,
and I sat up on my elbows

looking at the half-moons on my wrists.
Once I heard the word *fuck*
I never forgot it.

I stood in the mirror, gargling,
and that's when I realized
my Easter dress was horrendous

but that certain words
looked great against my teeth.

A NEW ILK OF MILK

Sometimes I take off my bra,
look at myself in the mirror,
and think—I'd like to nurse the masses.

Yeah, you heard me right.
Just walk up to hungry people
and say, *Want milk?*
Like saying *Wanna cigarette?*
Wanna beer? Only I'd be offering triple bock
breast milk. 100% unfiltered, unpasteurized,
unhomogenized cow juice.
But from the real McCoy.

Like, I can produce this crazy cola
all on my own 'cuz I've got glands, man.

And what if I never have a real baby,
just you, baby, and these jugs go to waste?
Like spigots at a sink that never get turned,
like bottles of fine wine that never get drunk,
just ogled and jostled,
but never popped, never poured,
never appreciated for the vintage brew they truly are.
Get a glass, I'd say.

Or just get on your knees,
and open your mouth for a stream
of this sweet boisson of the season.
If America can have a love affair with sparkling wines,
why can't they just kiss the umbilicus
and lick the slick-n-kwik inner gin
of womenfolk's white McMother earth soda:
a sensational swill blended from the hops,
skip-and-a-jump away from Eve
who probably tickled Adam with her sweet-lovin'

Godmade EdenSoy.
You can bet that slippery snake
came down and wanted her to PBR it ASAP.

And soon, all the animals came two-by-two
(because she only had two nipples)
and those animals just suckled and gurgled and mooed,
falling asleep in her arms
until she became so popular they crowned her
Miss Universe—which is why
all those pageant contestants
have gargantuan public busts.

Milk: it's what's for dinner.
If you're lucky, I'll unbutton a button
and nothin' you've ever drunk
will taste so sweet and so cold.
Not even William Carlos Williams
could fathom the plums in this ice
chest.

Forget your Tang,
your Tab, your seltzers and spritzers.
I've got two straws right here.
I bet if you'd just run a race and all the Gatorade
was gone and my Minute-Made
was in your mouth, you'd guzzle it like O.J.
(now there's a man who should have been breast-fed),
but now that I've got you titillated
and curious and contemplating the consumption
of my Gyno-Guiness,

let me rethink this. This isn't *just* milk.
You can't just expect me
to lean over and douse your bran flakes.
You can't just come over here with your coffee cup
and expect a free slosh of cream.
Hell no, this dairy dream is going to cost you,
baby,

just a little something. Not cash,
but maybe
if you could bring a few tears to your eyes,
if you could find it in yourself to conjure
up a little brine, if you could sniffle
and whimper a little,
we could trade your juices for mine.
Go ahead. Cry, baby.

SEDUCTIVE PRODUCE

Imagine peaches,
the fine hair of their navels
pressing you toward a nude beach
where sprayers
bent toward lettuce
form moonbows
between your pecks. What I'm seeing
is your body ribboned
with basil, mustard greens, dill—
women squeezing
your knees, cheeks, thighs
as they refer to grocery lists.
Or you are on ice,
lemons wedged under each armpit
as you sit astride salmon and halibut,
perfect shrimp deveined
on a sample platter
as aisle managers swarm you.
We could stay in bed, eat cold orzo,
share the last piece of tempeh,
but the real lingerie
is in the lobster tanks.
Toes
are turning ripe
near the deli—all those wives in open-toed pumps
waiting on their rotisserie chicken.

Of course, we could defrost the lentil loaf,
rummage for tamari,
but what I see, lover,
is you going through the checkout line,
belly down across the scanner.
Your shoes off,
arms out,
your skin cool on the metal counter
as the cashier takes a deep breath,
flips back her hair,
and begins to ring numbers
into your shoulders,
her well-oiled fingers
moving deep
into the under-tofu of your flesh.

SCAT

The study or preoccupation
      with excrement
is not just a game for scavengers.
The distinctive odor
that an animal deposits on the ground
is a signal to others of its kind. Sportive, a musical movement.
Along the Mohawk River, dung
beatles   their bronzelike luster
become the basic monetary unit.
      In the East Village, this sphere of activity
is the current fashion scene.

The act of scattering resembles desire.

Our bodies produce
      small parts
that cannot be reunited. In secret,
or in private,

we eat voraciously, then expel
      burnt gases.
Parties form in the bathroom
around beautiful scenery,
doubts dispelled
in the improvised nonsense of scat.

Sometimes, there is a schematic arrangement—
an intriguing design: Victor's long ragged wand
(an emblem of regal power),
     Claudine's series of canal
      boats. After supper,
Karl's tusk is iridescent,
       depending on certain minerals.

Other times it falls
in scentless scarves. There are variations
     in warmth and dearth.
The cowardly braggart is easily vanquished
by shitting a scarab-shaped amulet.

But mostly, it is Pedro's
small Belgian dog who excretes art
on the carpet. We gather
round a miniature railroad for carrying passengers,
a system of correlated things,
schematized,
       diagrammed
   like jazz.

NOT WANTING A CHILD

. . . The river / has been everywhere, imagine, dividing, discerning, . . .
—Jorie Graham

How hard is it to dam a river with your finger?
Every human lingers on, shoving half a code into a nematode.

But a prairie is burnt, then grows back
twice as full of foxglove. No seeding.

Isn't that one wooden match love? The grass aflame,
swallows taking flight through smoke—

two mating dragonflies slightly
charred. Sooner or later, the earth renews itself

without rolling eggs down a gully.
I am not a pulley

raising my proud helixes like a flag.
I'd rather burn this bed and let the rain clean out this room.

Eventually, a new bed would sprout—
first the posts: four equidistant wood mushrooms,

then slowly the mattress, like low-lying wheat.
When the fog lifted, there would be sheets

and shadows of pillows where our heads had been.
Here, let us throw our heads back to love long and bravely

without the dream of farmers,
grimly cultivating a field in erect hats.

Every parent is an elongated infant, yes,
but not all of us need replicate desire

or even deep pleasure in order to feel
that we have left our manifest yes on earth. Lie down,

lie down with me in this burning bed.

MUSIC FOR LILIES

Could be my breast's slip cover.
Could be the heart's umbrella.
Or a lunular truth, mouth, moth.
The generous luggage of how one day opened,
petulant but not petulant enough.
Perhaps I misunderstood Phaedra
who fell in love with her stepson,
night and day becoming lingerie, periodically.
Petulant, but not petulant
enough, lying by the base of an Orangina bottle
hand on the throat of,
lips on the mouth of,
the stem of which *is* the suede in persuade.
Youth and age, two petals
closed like curtains. The lusty center
still intact, petulant. Human.
Could be my own baby's plug, lung.
Could be my own funereal comma
collapsed like an open-and-shut case of daylight,
a minute winnowed down to this weak sleeve,
this wave of melodrama,
a yellow drama beneath a recycled *vahs*.
Could be a worn stocking
that keeps bunching above the shoe.
Could be the last sunset, or yesterday's keening.
Peel it back to remember:
jealousy, temptation, despair.
Not Pandora's box, but her knapsack.
Not a hummingbird or the yolk,
but a humanbird, sweetly post-titter,
post-listless, post-Las Vegas,
a glitter strip of sinew on a dull-green place mat.
Post-rife, post-wife, mother,
Other. Casing now, raw silk of rasbora.
The day lady died (a lily in her hair),

leaned against the table, fried,
fell, unrousable; each day I grow wide-eyed
on the drug of having lived
one day longer, then grow down.
A flower—ach, the unsucculent polemic.
To rise, to go achingly into the sky as pollen,
a quip of skin left behind, if that:
brief myth, brief sheath,
aftermath
of a quick, bright empire.

THE RECOURSE OF DRIFTING

Perhaps deep down we were trying to pretend we were pretending.
—Jose Emilio Pacheco

Year after year, somehow you never interrupted me.
Now you are furiously intact. The power of our enormous distance
has escaped, bitten me. How many hours of gnawing are left?
Stashed in the closet, letters on blue paper
stand up in the night, head for the beach.
I am raw in that dismal hotel with the salty walls,
tourists singing Jimmy Buffet all night long.
Maybe this is the terrible deep,
a backwashed siren serving you in pill form, lethal.
Water swept into the cabanas, remember?
And there we were, stick figure clinging to stick figure;
crass doodle, it seemed we would always stay that way,
drying into one another. Barnacles.
I will never know what you tried to tell me underwater,
though my memory fishes for it with a three-year-old bone.
Some nights the phone rings,
and the god of the sea is there. Other times, the wires buzz
and faintly, very faintly, I hear a parrot
bawling like a baby.
Now I am the pitchfork's wife with ten mouths to feed,
but no children. Hunger transmits its frequency for you
through hair, bones, blood.
I think how we spend all our lives learning to die.
What a fool I was
to think I could evaporate,
lazily forgetting the catastrophe of your body
washing up against me.

MADAME DELUXE

When you are guillotined
your head goes on thinking for two minutes.
If I were guillotined, my head
would remember this:
a drag queen dressed like a barnyard hen,
her tiara slightly to the side.
Red lips moving over something
thick and pre-sung in the smoke.

The room holds all of this in a waterglass,
in the sheen off caviar,
glitter, and jockstraps,
waxed legs and nose trimmers,
deep cups full of foam,
but also this: a white bird rising with my wrists in its beak.

When my head is cut off from your body,
I think of you dancing around the fallen axe.
Your wings beating, your eyelashes
batting but you can't
lift up in those heels.

It's the body that stops feeling,
forgets, but the eyes still see
your red stockings. The nose knows the sweat.
The ears hear the needle scratch your jazz.

My teeth will remember
your teeth like little drawers of silver
fish. My brain will taste
a row of shining sardines in brine.
At night, my lips will come to kiss
your dazzling neck.

FROM MADAME DELUXE'S DISCOUNT BIN

What I've learned about religion
is that you can get it through sex.

What I've learned about beauty
is that it glows in the dark,
is sometimes lubricated.

The speed of light
has something to do with blondes.

There are nervous wrecks
about to pull over to a shoulder.

There are "sinners" and most of them eat chocolate.

The drinking age
is the year wine was born.

A good body is hard because it has sat out
a long time. If it's brown,

flush it down. What I've discovered
is that there are different drummers,
but few of them are women.

Oxymorons
are dumb girls with clear skin.

That's what's good for the gander. Listen:
love is a polite way of saying *all right already.*

Life is a little wet spot. We should all
have red plaques over our bedroom doors:

Thanks for stopping,
Please come again.

POST-DELUXE

You have come to the right place.

Let me show you to your deluxe abode.

No need to stand up,

just look at the olive in the bottom

of your glass: that briny eye.

You wonder where the extra virgin

lives—she's inside, sleeping in

her olive tomb, her body

wrapped in flames.

You have come to the right place,

the in-between address

of moods. Be a darling,

take me from this lounge to my room

and tie me up before I can think of ways

to swallow you.